Life's

Wrong

Turns

A Book
by

Robert L. Harris

HATCHBACK Publishing
Genesee MI

Life's Wrong Turns
©2018 Robert L. Harris

Published by
HATCHBACK Publishing
Genesee, Michigan 48437
Since 2005

The views, opinions and words expressed in this book are those of the author and do not necessarily reflect the position of HATCHBACK Publishing LLC or its owners

ISBN 978-1-948708-14-2

Printed in USA
10 9 8 7 6 5 4 3 2 1

For Worldwide Distribution

Dedication

Much like everything in life, I thank God. Just believing in Him makes all things possible.

This book is dedicated to my Mom and Dad, Robert and Ozzie Harris who are now in Paradise

To my Daughter, Tracy and Husband, Curtis

To my Grandchildren:
London, Dakota, Denver and Sicily

Table of Contents

Prologue

Life's Wrong Turn is about turns we may sometimes take of all the different avenues we travel requiring decisions along the way. I hope to share with you some of life's wrong turns I'm sure each of us may take at one point or another. We all would like to believe that we are on the right road. I mean, who purposely gets on the wrong one? Hardly anyone.

Life is much like a highway, as you travel, you hope to reach your destination. You plot a course and begin your journey. Many times, it goes just as you have planned it. However, there may be a time you take the wrong turn which takes you where you did not intend to go. That wrong turn does not necessarily have to be all bad, you simply get back on course. Most of the time, there is no real harm. However, some wrong turns can be a danger. Many people have gotten in trouble this way. Much like the movie, some turns may land you in a situation you don't want to be in.

I hope to explain the decisions we have to make in everyday life. You can't go a day without having to decide on something. Sometimes the wrong turns we take could be bad although we try to be careful not to do this. But occasionally we do make bad choices. One should realize some may greatly affect you and some maybe a life changer. So when you come to that fork in life's' road and you really may not know which way to choose, choose the right way. You may be okay. The other, there is no telling what is in store for you.

1 *A Wrong Turn*

We all have ups, downs, setbacks and turn arounds. We have good decisions, bad ones, let downs, disappointments and surprises. We travel many avenues in a lifetime. From the day you are born, only you live out your destiny. While you are young, and haven't gotten out in the world, its' your parents that steer you in directions you may take the rest of your life. While most parents do their best at raising their kids, kids stand a greater chance according to the good things they were taught.

Not all parents may be considered good ones. They fail at good parenting not teaching facts of life. They don't teach life lessons. It's unfair as well as unfortunate any kid not be taught the realities of life. It is like a mother bear who does not teach her cub to hunt, once out on its own, the cub does not stand a chance. In fact, you can put a five hundred pound bear that was born in captivity loose in the wilderness and he would starve. A rabbit could outwit him. Why? No one taught him right from wrong. The very same principle applies with kids. And from the lack of being taught, that child may be, for the rest of life, making one wrong turn after another. Please don't misunderstand me, no amount of good teaching may guarantee that any child have a trouble free life. I figure it is better to be taught than not.

Some people take a wrong turn and keep on going. Probably because they had no guidance. Everything we see and hear may help make up our minds when we must decide to do something. Many things we take in and are influenced by come from subliminal messaging.

Subliminal messaging are sensory stimuli below an individual's threshold for conscious perception. Whether we know it or not messaging may help control our lives and decisions we make. We do both good and bad because of it. Take a child for instance. By the time that child is three years old, they know about McDonalds because they hear it all the time. They will say, "I want to go to McDonald's." Why? Their commercials are aimed at children. They send out subliminal messages kids will associate with. For a kid, McDonald's is the place to go. You don't often hear a kid say, "I want to go to Arbys."

We take in information, it is then stored in the mind and processed to be used later. It is sort of like the "go to page". When we need to do something we go to that page, some of which are intakes of subliminal messaging. I know that it works. For example, a long time ago, I was going home from work about midnight. My every intent was to go straight home, a drink was the furthest thing from my mind. I came to a stoplight and while sitting there I looked up at a billboard. There was thing guy in a tuxedo holding a drink and a pretty woman. I then thought...you know a drink would be nice. Off to the club I went. I wanted to be like the guy in the tuxedo. After a few drinks and looking for that pretty woman, which I did not find, on the way home I got pulled over by the police. There is no need to tell the rest. If only I had not looked at the stupid billboard. Be careful of the subliminal because it can be misleading, get you in trouble. And be especially careful if you live in a certain neighborhood that seemed to have billboards and churches not far apart. One for damnation, one for salvation.

2 *Either or Methods*

There is nothing any of us do that may reassure our outcome. Where life's rivers flow, no one can really tell. Either way it is you and you alone who is held accountable for your life. Good or bad, right or wrong, it is you that reap rewards or suffer the consequences of your ways. In a world where you are expected to be responsible, versatile, dependable, logical, philosophical, accountable, intellectual and presentable can be a lot to confirm to. For the lack of any of these character traits may be what is wrong with any of us.

I do the best I can and hope that gets it. True, some people can't get with this program and deviate from much of it, okay. Let's hope the way you see and do things work for you, no one can say it won't work. Not every way is right, not every way is wrong. Individuality, as far as I am concerned is the best course. Until you sort things out where you understand what's going on, go it alone, seeking advice along the way.

Influenced

All people are influenced by all types of information gathered along the way, then they put this information to work which may help or hinder. Personally, it is my belief that there is too much bad information out there, which make people do all sorts of things. You may be in trouble if you are unable to distinguish good from bad. Our prisons are full of people who were influenced by bad information. Sadly, I feel it is the kids who are greatly affected and will ultimately pay the price. I strongly recommend, if you love them, do your very best at teaching right from wrong. Explain the real world and how it works.

I believe a good method when teaching kids is the either or method. It simply means, either you do a certain thing correctly or there will be repercussions or consequences. It is not a harsh method because it teaches them at an early age they are responsible for what they do and they will have to answer for it.

I my military days, my first night in boot camp, we didn't finish getting processed and sworn in until very late at night. Finally hitting the sack tired and worn out, after a few hours of sleep, the alarm goes off for us to rise and shine. My thoughts were...you've got to be kidding! We just got into bed! They can't really mean for us to get out of the bed. So I laid there thinking it was a joke. This two hundred pound drill sergeant grabbed me out of the bed and slung me across the room. That helped me to realize the either or effect get of bed when we say so or get tossed out. I also realized this is no joke and these people are not playing. To this day I am grateful and I learned from that experience. In my life it's helped me with some ways of seeing and doing things. To this day I still see things in an either or manner. If you have a job, either you go to work or you get fired. Either you pay your mortgage or get thrown out. Either take care of your car or it breaks down. Either choose the criminal life, maybe go to jail or steer clear of things that may put you there.

I once worked with a guy who had a son who wanted a puppy. The dad wasn't crazy about the idea. However, he gave in on conditions that the son would clean behind the dog. As time went on, the son came up with every excuse to not live up to what was agreed. Excuses like, I'm late for school, I've got to do homework, or I've got to go to baseball practice. The dad found himself often cleaning the mess. The dad wanted to get rid of the dog because of this. By this time, the son had grown attached and he didn't want to hurt his son in this way. Finally, being frustrated, the dad decided a way that would make his son live up to what was agreed. Each time the son would make an excuse, the son would come home and the crap would be in a plastic bag in his bed. At first, the son and his mother would have a fit, especially the wife. However, the dad was undeterred by anything his wife or son had to say. The dad finally made a breakthrough. Either you stick to the agreement or the crap will be in your bed.

The mess finally became the son's top priority. Nothing stood in the way...I'll do my homework after I clean behind my pal.

I believe that may have taught the son that you can't get by on excuses. The dad may have made his son a better person. If you ask me, this is either or at its finest.

My dad had a method with his kids that seemed to have worked well. I don't know about the rest of my sisters and brothers, so I'll just say it worked well for me. When you did something wrong, you never knew how he would take it and what he might do. Sometimes the discipline would be he would say absolutely nothing...leaving you to wonder. You would be left surprised because you just knew you had something coming. You would feel like you have been given a second chance at life. Other times you would feel you better run for your life, that's if you wanted to live. Sometimes it was something you did, that wasn't as bad as the thing you did you felt you should have really been disciplined for, he would let you slide. He kept you in a wondering state of mind. You didn't want to take any chances unleashing his wrath. If my father said be home by ten o'clock, if you have to, break speed records to be home by ten. One time I went somewhere and got lost. Finally making it home around midnight, which was two hours past my curfew, I was thinking I was just dead. When I get home my dad was up and waiting. He asked me where I had been and I told him I got lost.

He then replied, "A fellow, every now and then gets lost. Good you found your way home. Go to bed. Get ready for school."

I then realized the real compassion my dad had for raising his kids and that it wasn't entirely all about discipline. At the same time, I began to understand to work with him, abide with him, he's got a hard job and teaching eleven kids can't be all easy.

My dad was the charter of his home. Many things revolved around him. He had this "stay on my good side and everything will be alright." He conveyed this and that' the side I wanted to be on. It was safer. If you could accomplish this, it was an indication you must be doing something right. I guess that was his way of letting you know if you were going to the right or to the left. He figured right to be a better choice.

Except for my mom, his word was law. Live by it or get your feelings hurt. I will say my dad had a way that put down insubordination. He simply gave you two choices, either or. He was viewed by all of his kids as a real man. Up until the day he died, he was unchallenged by his children. Great job Dad!

My mom was somewhat different as far as discipline goes. I mean she could be all for giving, although you stood a better chance with her, yet I learned to not underestimate her. She was a bit more understanding. You could sometime even con her. As far as she was concerned, we were all her babies.

But one day I went too far. I awakened the real discipline ways she had, which far exceeded anything my father ever did. I was coming home from school one day and I got into an argument with a much older senior lady. I used profanity to get her told. I walked away thinking I got her straight. It made me feel bigger and badder. I stood up for myself. I got home later to find that same lady was at my house talking to my mom.

I heard her say, "I know you are a good Christian woman and I know you try and raise your kids. But that son of yours cursed me out."

My mother replied, "Don't worry. I got this." She then looked at me and said, "Boy, I'm getting ready to make a better person out of you."

Then came the worst whopping I ever had in my life. She used that belt with the skills of a surgeon. I saw a side of my mom I never knew existed. She was right for it was that very day, to disrespect and elderly person was completely gone from my young mind.

I also found respect branched out in other areas as well. To this day I try to respect people. Although I have done this, I won't lie, I find it hard to use profanity around women. I do my best to refrain from it. I was on a road if which I had gotten away with it, may have led me to believe it was okay to use profanity on women. What she did was everlasting.

My mom put me on the right road. My mom was right. She did make a better person out of me. Thank you, Mom.

3 *Everyone Takes a Wrong Turn*

All of us take, a may continue to take a wrong turn throughout our lives. Young or old matters little when we're faced with something we must decide on or we may be unsure or uncertain what to do. Time will determine that for all of us. Just as things we do correctly, there are also mistakes. That's what life consists of. No one is perfect, if so, I would love meeting them. They may help by explaining a few things I need to know.

The truth is, the best we can do is to be careful of choices and hope we have done the right thing. We may use knowledge or past experiences to help make up our minds. The more knowledge you have gives you an edge, as opposed to someone who has little. It pays to have an open mind to something you may learn. Closed minded people do not get far. Once you have closed your mind, nothing else enters thus cutting you off from the latest news.

No one should feel bad about wrong turns, that's life. It may be something that helps to correct you because improvements are a good thing. If you could speak with someone who might be considered a success, they might admit some of their mistakes. Because of their success, you may not realize some of life's wrong turns they have taken. It could be many. You may think, how is that possible when everything they touch turn into gold? Well, like everyone else, their life consisted of trial and error. Have no misconceptions that they made no mistakes. They may have even done dumb things. Their difference is that somewhere along the way, they got it right. They learned what they may have been doing wrong and corrected it. Time, for anything we may do, answers all we do. You may have your answer tomorrow or twenty years from now.

At the time we do certain things, we may not know if it is right or wrong. Sort of like a bet. You believe you have a hunch, you have made a good bet. You gamble, you hope you win. You believe you are going to win otherwise you never would have placed the bet. Only later will tell if your hunch was right. There is no sure thing when placing a bet. If there was, we would all be rich.

The same principle applies when we make these turns. The more of what you decide is well thought out, or the more you know on a subject, you will stand a better chance of knowing you have done the right thing. Seek knowledge for it may help you better decide. Common sense may be your best bet. It may help to aid you. Maybe more than a college education. There is a term, "Educated fool." That is an educated person who does not use common sense. They rely on their education more than common sense. Education and common sense should go hand in hand.

If you are educated you shouldn't rely on one and dismiss the other.

4 *Life Changers*

We should be careful with what you do. No one can get it right all of the time. However, you should know certain things may follow you for life. I knew someone who was caught stealing when they were sixteen years old. Thirty years later, there was a job this person really wanted. They could not get the job because of petty theft.

Some people, especially young people, don't realize it is important to have a clean record. It may be silly that some petty things someone may do may block something they want to do. Our prisons are full of people who are there for something petty. Once in the system, you now belong to the system. You may never make a turn around. And don't get three strikes, you're out.

The truth is, people are gullible. Each of us are capable of doing something horrendous. It makes little difference if you are rich or poor, black or white, educated or a drop out.

You may be successful or a failure. You may be powerful and influential. You may hold public office or be the greatest entertainer in the world. You still may be gullible. No one escapes this fact. Many things are within the souls and minds of people. Love, hate, greed, ambition, anger and sexual deviations are just a few that are contained within us.

Although we may not realize, some of us live within the seven deadly sins. Some of which may send you straight to hell. If you happen to be a restless soul, matters may be worse for you because you are never content. It may be hard for you to find peace.

Some of us want to stretch things to the limit, to the ultimate of nothing. Success does not guarantee you will find happiness. You may have made that beyond your reach because you are bewildered. You won't allow your mind to rest. You work against yourself. You don't allow good things to seep in. You are not grounded in the ways that count. What you are looking for may be just around the corner, thus making short work of your search.

I love watching someone's autobiography. I have done so for years. I like knowing what made them and what broke them. All too often I find that success was too much for them. They could not handle it. They would turn into their own worst enemy. They seem to look for excuses to not be happy, a mega star, and dead at forty-two. To be content, I believe is the best way. That's because you don't put too many demands on yourself. Simply put, you are not at war against you. After you have reached your highest plateau, you may not be able to top that. Try and enjoy your achievements and move on. Real happiness simply may be you are under no strains and pressure. You live in a comfortable home and you have friends. If you want to travel, you can afford to do so. You have a wonderful family. You are in love with someone and they are in love with you. You may not have millions but you are not exactly broke. Instead of reaching for the moon, reach for the clouds. That's still pretty high. As simple as this may sound, many don't have this. Uncomplicate things. Don't worry be happy. Leave all the rest alone. Don't be gluttonous.

Lately I have seen that many rich and powerful people are in the spot light for all of the wrong reasons. Some are the same people that want to give us life in the penitentiary without parole for something we did. Imagine that. You can't hardly watch the news without learning of all the different sexual accusations, and other crimes. An act that happened forty years ago is being brought to the surface. I wonder what did the accused think. Did they think they got away with it all? Or maybe they thought they could erase it from their minds like it never happened. They may have though because it seems they are above the law and some are sad to say. This is a good example of what's done in the dark will come to the light. It's got to be embarrassing. Didn't they realize if you dance to the music you must pay the piper? Somewhere they must have taken a wrong turn.

Stay true to yourself. Although the world may be full of scandal and deceit, not to mention all of the temptation, with things sometimes seeming hopeless, stay loyal to yourself. Try and steer clear without getting trapped in the madness because you may not be able to get out. If you feel like that's the way things are try to remain neutral. Don't think in ways that may be distorted. It may get you into trouble in the long run. Many people have little faith and commit to do some of the wrong things. If you choose to do what's right with just a little faith, if you put your mind to it, things may work for you. Even if it seems everyone else is doing bad things doesn't mean you have to. It takes a special person to see through all of the insanity. Many can't. You gamble when doing what's wrong. What's at stake is your life, don't throw it away. The world is waiting for you to make mistakes so you may be penalized. God did not give you life for you to spend it incarcerated. Look on the brighter side of darkness. Ask yourself do you want to go home or do you want to go to jail?

5 *Cell Phones*

Cell phones were intended as a convenient way to communicate. It's nice to be able to receive and place calls from practically anywhere. You are never out of reach if someone needs to contact you.

Convience, believe it or not, is not always a good thing. Anytime there is improper usage of anything, it defeat the purpose it was intended for. Sometimes people do just that! There is also abuse which goes against the intended purpose.

Cell phones, in my belief, is one of the main carriers of bad news, useless news, gossip, and all sorts of rumors. They make it easy to spread rumors and talk about people in a bad way. If you receive ten calls, I bet eight of those are some sort of problem or bad news. Many calls we receive does us absolutely no good. We seldom get great news. Many calls regulate you in ways some may not understand. When you receive a call, you must respond in one way or another.

A lot of people's lives have been set off by the usage of cell phones. Some have been distracted while driving and many have been killed or injured because of it. If you are not conscientious of this fact, it may be your silent enemy. People are preoccupied as well as possessed. Cell phones has become like a third hand for us. We rely on it for many things, not all good.

You can hardly have a conversation with someone before it is disrupted by a call or two. Some calls you can do without. If that call is not important, you should keep it short, especially if you are preoccupied with someone else. You could be on the brink of something important or special and before you know, it is disrupted by someone wanting to gossip. Some feed right into this. It is possible you may miss out on something good if you fail to understand.

Cell phones, in my opinion is one of the greatest regulators in our lives. We may not realize this, but we are controlled by them.

There is no escape from it. You can hardly watch a movie at home without being interrupted.

Many have taken wrong turns because of cell phones and it has wrecked people's lives. Criminal activities now has a different highway that keeps the business going because of phone calls which can be easily made for transactions. A lot of married people and relationships have run into all sorts of problems because of cell phones. It has caused confusion, arguments, distrust, tracking and sometimes untrue accusations.

Parents these days must now contend with the fact their child has a cell phone which may be misused, putting them in harm's way.

In sort, cell phones show us no mercy period. Cell phones don't care why we use them. It is not their job to care. It is the engine that controls lives. It is like a run-away train. You, the individual, should do better to understand this and help someone else.

I've advised a few people in relationships to stay off of that phone especially when your mate is around. Romance may have to take a backseat to a call and your mate may no longer be interested. That individual did not know how to prioritize and didn't realize that sometimes, one time can be too many. I know a thing or two because I've seen a thing or two. So in reality you may not have to worry about a man or woman taking your mate, a cell phone may do that. It does me good to know I am not the only one who sees it this way.

6 *Choose Your Friends*

Throughout life we may have many friends. There are friends of all sorts. There are those we may see every day. Even though we may not have much to do with them, other than speak and maybe talk about something, they are considered friends. There are those we may know from a distance, we may hardly even see them and they are friends. There are those we grew up with over the years. Then there are those who are in our lives on a regular basis. Most people have a need for friendship. There is absolutely nothing wrong with this. Who doesn't want to have a friend? Sometimes a good one may be hard to find. Like many other things, you should choose friends and associates carefully. I know it may be hard to know a friend and all too often we find out later, they were not really your friend. Depending on who we hang out with, some may be bad news for you. If they want to do things you don't believe in and you don't agree on - many people have gotten into trouble listening to a friend.

When I was younger, I had someone I hung out with and had done so for years. I thought I knew him. One day he hit me with the news he wanted to rob someone. I was shocked. Not only was I not raised that way, I didn't and still don't believe in robbery. He tried hard to get me to go along. He even told me I was afraid. He was right! There was nothing he could say to make me do this. There is no telling how that may have gone. I had no wish to find out. I couldn't do it and I even talked him out of it. He really should have considered me a real friend. I didn't want him to get into trouble. Some people can be so easily persuaded into doing something they really don't want to do. The person that convinces them really doesn't care what happens to the other person. Unless you take charge of what you will and won't do, you could get into trouble.

Like many things we do, we shop around for sales. We shop around for furniture, we certainly look for the better deal on cars. Friendship is no different. Choose carefully.

Try and steer clear of those you don't have much in common, for it may only cause friction. Steer clear of those who are hard to be around, it may keep you on edge. Be leery of the ones you seem to always have to do for, you may not be able to afford their friendship. Try and keep away from the ones that are so complicated and difficult. They should have an instruction manual to go along with them. The idea of friendship is that you get along, maybe aid each other should you need to, and share common ground. You don't need a lot of controversy that goes with friendship. Some friends may help to decide your fate. Don't be misled. Don't take the wrong turn.

7 *Setting Your Own Standards*

To set standers for yourself is a good thing. I doubt anyone can argue that. It means you won't go beyond boundaries you don't believe in. You name limits. You make self-care a priority. One must say no to things they do not believe in or know it's wrong. Things that don't go with the way you do things or the way you see things.

In life, there are many things we must decide on, what's best to do. You must understand what works for you. Many people have gotten into trouble because of their inability to say no to something they may not have wanted to do in the first place. They simply went along. No one every taught them that you can choose to be a leader but you should refuse to be a follower of misleading people.

I believe individuality is your best bet. Sometimes you may have to go it alone until you find something that fits. If it doesn't fit don't force it. It may be that certain kind of stubbornness that may sometimes work on your behalf. People can't help but to go with what they believe. Sometimes you may hear, "You are so stubborn." That's okay. If that's the way you are it simply means that you are not going to just listen to any one. You are not so easily moved. You just don't go along with any ole program. It means you must convience me otherwise or else move on. It has both it's up and down sides. However, you must stand on what you believe until proven wrong.

Once I did something incorrect for years believing I was doing right until someone showed me the error of my ways. It is at that point one should realize, you may have been a little stubborn, but that's it! Although you may have been wrong, you stay committed to what you believed. That was a good thing for you. But if someone has shown you a better way, it is at that point you should admit you were wrong. To not to do this only means you are stubborn in the worst way. This is not good.

Leaders and Followers

There is nothing wrong with listening to a good leader no matter who you might be. You may be wise to know they are a good leader and even humble yourself. They may have just the information you need to make your life better. If you have uncertainties about anything, it may remain with you because you had no one to help you clarify and see things correctly. A good leader may do this. Until this happens, you may be wrong about something all of your life. You are blessed to have a good leader you can learn from.

Just as there are good leaders, there are also bad leaders. You may live to regret it if you follow the wrong one. They may set you on a path of no return. Such as the Guyana tragedy, the *People's Temple*. Over nine hundred people lost their lives to a manipulator. A manipulator is simply a wolf in sheep's clothing. There are many. After they have gained your confidence, once it is over, you will have been had. You will find out many of the things you have believed that came from them are untrue. They sold you a bill of goods you never received. These are people that have selfish motives. Personal gain is what they are after. You are just the prey. They may offset your life in a way which you never fully recover. And if you do so, you may bear scars of that experience.

So if you should detect this type of deceit in someone, allow them to go no further. Cut them off at the ankle, which is where it may start. If you don't, then it progresses to the knees. Then the waist, then the heart, finally the mind. When it goes that far, you are all theirs. They will then take you up the downside of reality. Don't go along for the ride. Pass that one on.

8 *The Course that You Take*

Some of the things I have talked about thus far is to explain how we have learned to think and where it all began. As we travel along life's highways, which are many, we make decisions on a lot of things. Most of what we decide is simple. It does not require major thinking. Even if we decide wrong, it may not be that serious and may not alter your life. However, there are decisions that we make that may change your life entirely. It's the bad ones, if bad enough, in the long run, may ultimately help cause your annihilation.

There are two types of choices, good as well as bad. When you decide on things that enhances your life, it's a good thing. Ever hear anyone say, "This was the best decision I ever made." I have been able to say that a few times myself. It may be the good decision to further your education, or lose weight, go on a diet, quit smoking, make a good investment, move to a better location, or to not do drugs. These may be good choices that may better your life and just may change things for you entirely. Overnight you may go from one existence to the next, based on what you decide. When you have to make what may be a difficulty choice, it may be a good thing to talk with someone who may be familiar with the subject. They may have already had experience in that area. Maybe give yourself a little edge. Get an idea of what you may be up against.

It puzzles me how some young, as well as old people, go out and do something for the first time and don't ask for advice from someone who has maybe done it a dozen times. They buy a house for the first time, yet they have an uncle who has done it many times and don't ask for advice. If you confide in that person, maybe you might make a better choice.

I had a friend who bought his first house. He paid cash and he paid the asking price. Didn't anyone ever teach this guy the fine art of haggling? In fact, most people raise the price of what they want because some may try and talk them down. Once he told me I was like, "You gave them the asking price? You didn't try to pay less?" This is not trying to pay less on a new TV, that I understand. But this was a house that's over a hundred thousand dollars. He didn't realize he had cash and could have probably paid thousands of dollars less than the asking price. I guarantee they would have taken it. He probably didn't realize this and never bothered to ask anyone.

Many of us have resources we don't use, such as a source of advice. What a waste. Many people do it this way, they will tell you after the fact. Then you are left to say, "You did what? You paid what?"

Even if you ask someone's advice, you are the one who ultimately decide what's best. That is the beauty of it. You were clever enough to at least ask. And by asking someone, it may help you not to make the wrong turn.

Then there are the turns that leaves little doubt you may have taken the wrong one.

This may cause a problem for you when you make a conscious choice or you simply may not at that time realize the decision you made may not have been a good one. It may have even been a stupid one. Stupidity has its place. It's like a scale that balances smart on one end and stupid on the other. Stupidity is sort of like an easy payment plan. Be stupid today, pay tomorrow.

You may do something stupid today and years later, it catches up to you. You see this all the time. You may take a wrong turn when you decide to drop out of high school, when you decide to hang with the wrong crowd, when you marry someone you should know is no good for you - you should know you should be with someone who is good to and for you. Other wrongs turns are when you consciously decide to do drugs, or when you engage in criminal activity that can put you behind bars for life. Is there anything good to be said for any of this? I don't think so.

It may be frightful to realize how a life can change. Any life can change at any given time. If there is no resistance, a change may do you more harm than good. You are responsible for your actions. I recommend if you run into anything you may be a little confused about, or you simply don't know quite what to do, talk to someone who may help. They might help you make better decisions. Although, some of us believe we know everything and may feel we don't have to ask anyone. Truth be told, we may not know all of what we think we know, in comparison to all we should know.

It is all out there for us, a mountain of choices. Only you may decide. There are rewards in it for you making good choices. It will make you feel better, the other, you don't feel so good. Aspire to do what you should do.

9 *Prepare for the Unexpected*

There are many situations in life that either help or cause us to have something we may be unprepared to deal with. Some of it can be so bad that the best you can do is pray for a miracle. It may be that something you previously did. When you did it, at that time, you may not have realized it may come back at you. You may not have realized what you did was incorrect. It may have been a miscalculation, or maybe you did something and hoped you got away with it. Believe it or not, we have to answer for most everything we do. It's like there is an eye in the sky that seems to watch us all. When the time comes around to answer it may catch you when you least expect it or can't afford it. And now whatever it may be is staring you in the face. You have to do something and you are right. You have to answer.

It has been my experience it's the unexpected that may happen when you least expect it. It could be a game changer for you. For example, many people receive mail from their energy service that may make them want to faint. They didn't expect such a large bill. One reason is they never learned strategies to not get shocking mail. In the summer your bill may be lower because you are not running a furnace which makes your bill higher. The summer months are the times to take advantage of that fact. Cut your pilot light on your furnace and save in other ways like, cutting that porch light off. Many people don't do this. They don't realize each day it costs and they are paying money for this. I've seen this one where someone has their central air on when it is only seventy degrees. It will cost around two thousand dollars more in the winter than it does during the summer. The money you are spared in the summer should be put aside for the winter. That is if you want to get a grip.

You should think this way, your energy service provider is one company. Some might agree you need to be tactful. That's if you don't want mail that will send you into a frenzy. The short story, take advantage of summer to be used for the winter.

Through my years, I have learned to realize this and other facts of life. If you don't want your world turned upside down, tactics may be required.

Sometimes, you have to be aware that you may be in fear of the mail you will receive. I've gotten bad news in the mail that has rocked my world. Once I was going to do something and I got a letter that changed all that. That letter did not go with anything that I planned. It was a game changer. It was nothing I expected neither was I prepared for it.

You get mail and it may be from the IRS saying you owe them money. Not a little but a lot. You think you must have done something that was incorrect. You may even believe this is a mistake. A large amount of money like five thousand dollars. You may think this can't be right...where am I going to get this type of money from? Whatever it is...you must now deal with it. This may cause you to have to scramble and scrape and put together money you don't have. This one cannot be ignored.

This may be typical. I am sure many have received mail that simply devastated them. The unexpected and the unprepared for.

Whatever one does may come back in their mailbox. There was something they did that was wrong and now they must pay for it.

Over the years I have paid close attention to this one. I hope to share this reality. Believe it or not, the mail you receive tells a lot about you and how you handle your affairs. It took me years to see this way. Don't take that turn that two years from now may deliver you bad news mail. That is mail you can do without. That is mail that simply breaks your heart, have you in tears, takes what little money you have, offsets things for you, may cause you to lose sleep, be angry and go broke.

I admit this may be an unusual way of looking at it but it is nevertheless true. Try your best to make sure you get beneficial mail. Mail that says you have been approved rather than denied.

This is an indication, good news mail means you must be doing something right.

10 *Growing Up in Chicago*

Growing up in Chicago was fun. As a kid my mom and dad took us downtown around Christmas time. It was nice. Everything was all lit up. Christmas lights and decorations were everywhere. People were so friendly. I thought I was in Wonderland. On State Street there were a lot of different movie theaters that smelled of popcorn. The restaurants were no different. As you walked along there were good smells that made you want to stop and eat.

At age eight, I loved Chicago. I thought there was no place like it. As time went on, things began to change. Suddenly there were drugs, gangs and guns everywhere. At first I may have been a little sheltered from some of it because of the way my parents ran their home. Eventually, I was all in. I saw many things that were horrific. Violence and chaos was everywhere. Going to school there were fights all the time. This all seemed normal.

Depending on which side of town you lived, things were either better or worse. There were different sides of town that you dared not go to.

When I was younger, I was all over Chicago. I had an uncle who had a carpet business. I would sometimes go with him on different jobs. Sometimes we were in very exclusive neighborhoods. This helped me to see how the other side lived and that it wasn't all poverty. You knew you were in a posh neighborhood when you would see chipmunks. To this day, I have never seen a chipmunk in an average neighborhood, only squirrels.

I grew up and ran in a circle of nine friends. We even called ourselves forming a little gang. It didn't amount to much at the time. It just seemed the thing to do. We were pretty good guys. I knew each one of them pretty well. As time went on, some of them began to drift into dangerous areas. Some began to go to jail. Some began to do drugs.

Some began to take complete wrong turns. I saw my friends begin to dissipate before my eyes. There were so many ways you could go wrong. All of the sudden, Chicago seemed to have gone crazy. You never knew what would happen next. I believe I may have been spared from some of all the dangerous and crazy things happening. At sixteen, I got an after school job which helped to keep me off of the street. I wanted to work all I could because I felt it helped me to stay out of trouble. Whenever I was confronted in terms of doing something wrong, because of my job and spending time with my uncle it kept me out of trouble. Not to mention my dad, who took me and my brother to Wrigley's Field to watch baseball games. Because of this, I had more to stand on. It made it easier to say no.

It also helped that I didn't come from a criminal source. My dad always told me, "Boy, be your own person. Don't let anyone make up your mind for you." What he said resonated with me.

At eighteen I joined the Navy removing myself altogether. I am not saying I didn't do things but somehow I was able to draw the line when doing things which would cause me to get in real trouble or go to jail.

Out of my nine friends, seven are dead. There is only me and one other left. I saw him about five years ago. We talked about the old days. It was good to know he felt the same as I did at that time about what was happening. He didn't like it any more than I did.

Even though your surroundings may be chaotic, you can get out if you want. You must first be man enough to know what is best for you. Don't let the boy overpower the man in you.

11 *Young People*

Young people have most of their lives ahead of them. The fact that they are young makes them more prone to mistakes. Unlike us old geezers who have traveled many of life's highways, and may have taken many wrong turns, nevertheless we survived and may have grown a little wiser.

Young people really do have a lot of choices they must make. They must decide if they want to further their education or dropout altogether. They must decide what they want to do with the rest of their lives. They must decide on what friends they want to hang out with taking a path that might take them somewhere or a path that may harm them. They must make the decision whether they are going to be in a gang or not. This may not be easy because of some of the wrong messages they take in, many may go astray. Sometimes they are just too young to understand.

Take a young person that has a baby. For both the male and the female, it is a life changer. Most are not ready. Suddenly there is this baby and they are no more than babies themselves. Who can honestly say young people know what to do? For the female, she is a mom at sixteen. She must now try to do the best she can with little or no support. The dad has run off somewhere. He's young and has things he wants to do. She must now put her education on hold. Sometimes forever. She must rely on others for help. The guy, in most cases is no help. At his age, he probably has no skills and no job therefore he isn't much help at all. Depending on who he has the child by, there may be now be "baby momma, baby daddy drama" that they both have to contend with. If the woman puts him on child support and the guy has no way to pay, before he reaches twenty-five years old, he is twenty-five thousand dollars in the rear. God forbid he has two or three more children.

A lot of children are not planned. They are not what we would call a "love child." It is better if a baby is something that they both wanted, planned and prepared for otherwise some men may feel getting a job is pointless. The Friend of the Court may take everything. Many people's lives gets turned around when this happens. So with no real means to make money, some people believe they have no choice, they turn to crime.

Having a baby at a young age may be the turn that offsets whatever you may want to do. Young people may not understand this. That's unfortunate. They really can't be faulted. It's just one of many things they get caught up in. A wrong turn at sixteen years old can keep you on a course for life. Take heed. Allow yourself time to mature a little. There is no rush. Don't try and live all of your life in one day.

Epilogue

I would love that everyone who reads this book enjoys it. I am honest to say I am hoping to reach out to younger people It is my hope that younger people are able to read and understand some of the things I have talked about. It may be because of something they read, they may latch onto something that may help them along the way. I hope they may understand to be careful with choices, choose their friends wisely, and to not make hasty moves. If I could reach one young person, it is worth it.

All I have written about I believe to be true. I realize I may have taken many wrong turns. People may have regrets about the choices they have made. There should be no real shame in it. The deed has been done. It is what we do. We decide on matters just as there were wrong decisions, I am sure there were many good ones. It is not all bad. All you have to do is correct yourself at every opportunity. You can do so or stay the same.

Take it easy, you will be surprised at what happens once you gain control of your mind.

It's okay to realize where you have gone wrong. Realizing is part of your growth.

One of my regrets is that I did not do twenty years in the Navy. If I had, I could have retired at the age of thirty-eight with a full pension. Still young enough to do other things, work or start a career doing something I really wanted to do.

Thinking back, I had fun in the service. There were constant travel all at the government's expense. The food was great, there was no mortgage and I certainly had the best medical plan. I had education if I wanted it and I was surrounded by friends. I was able to go to places where in a lifetime I would have never been able to go. Things that I learned was unlimited. There was always excitement and always something to do.

Some would say you may be killed in the service. This may be true. You could also be killed while walking your doggie.

The reason I didn't stay was simple. I was young and foolish. I failed to realize at that time I would have regrets later. I took a wrong turn. I was learning to be structured which I now believe was a good thing. I was part of the biggest organization in the world. Back then I did not see it that way. I believed at that time, I had too many demands I had to conform to. They wanted me to get up each morning at five o'clock!

Working for General Motors, I felt I could be my own person and do what I wanted. I never really realized that in the real world, you still must conform.

You cannot do what you want if you have a job. A lot may be expected from you. As long as you are in this life, you have to answer to someone whether it is a drill sergeant, your boss at work or your wife. You must answer.

In the real world, it may take years. It is an uphill climb to establish, to gain, and to maintain a life where you are okay with your status. In the service, much of this is done for you. This all depends on people's point of view. This is mine and you are entitled to yours.

This is why I know young people can sometimes be irrational. Many things are not well thought out. Some don't see the big picture. Some may make impulsive choices. Some are eager to prove themselves right. And like me, may regret their decisions years later.

I am sure most of us have one big regret in life. Something that we may now believe to have been the wrong choice, bad decision or wrong turn. I have told you mine. There is no shame in it. It is simply the turn I took.

We still may be faced with roads we may take and those we shouldn't. Only now we may be capable of making a better choice and may help someone else with theirs.

Thanks for reading. I hope that it helps someone understand. Don't be hasty in your decision, especially when there is no rush to make up your mind. Be subtle and allow yourself to make a good choice.

Remember fools rush in where wise men dare not go. Pray for peace, love, prosperity and understanding. Amen

Author Bio

A Vietnam veteran, serving time in the Navy as a gunners mate, Robert Harris retired from General Motors after thirty years of service and now operates his own landscaping business.

Born in Chicago, Illinois, Robert now resides in Saginaw, Michigan. He is the proud father of a lovely daughter and four beautiful grandchildren.

To contact Robert for information or speaking engagements email:

rharris44.rhh@gmail.com

www.ingramcontent.com/pod-product-compliance
Lightning Source LLC
Chambersburg PA
CBHW051709090426
42736CB00013B/2607